MAR    2014

MIDLOTHIAN PUBLIC LIBRARY

3 1614 00163 2398

MIDLOTHIAN
PUBLIC LIBRARY

W9-ANP-618

* Smithsonian

# A WORLD WAR I

BY PAMELA DELL

MIDLOTHIAN PUBLIC LIBRARY
14701 S. KENTON AVE.
MIDLOTHIAN, IL 60445

CAPSTONE PRESS
a capstone imprint

Capstone Press,
1710 Roe Crest Drive
North Mankato, Minnesota 56003
www.capstonepub.com

Copyright © 2014 by Capstone Press, a Capstone imprint. All rights reserved.
No part of this publication may be reproduced in whole or in part, or stored
in a retrieval system, or transmitted in any form or by any means, electronic,
mechanical, photocopying, recording, or otherwise, without written permission
of the publisher.

The name of the Smithsonian Institution and the sunburst logo
are registered trademarks of the Smithsonian Institution.
For more information, please visit www.si.edu.

Capstone would like to thank Kealy Wilson, Smithsonian Institution Product
Development Manager, and the following at Smithsonian Enterprises: Ellen
Nanney, Licensing Manager; Brigid Ferraro, Vice President, Education and
Consumer Products; Carol LeBlanc, Senior Vice President, Education and
Consumer Products.

**Library of Congress Cataloging-in-Publication Data**
Dell, Pamela.
 A World War I timeline / by Pamela Dell.
 pages cm. — (Smithsonian war timelines)
 Includes index.
 Summary: "In timeline format, covers the chronology of major events of World
War I"— Provided by publisher.
 ISBN 978-1-4765-4159-4 (library binding)
 ISBN 978-1-4765-5179-1 (paperback)
 1. World War, 1914-1918—Chronology—Juvenile literature. I. Title. II. Title:
World War 1 timeline. III. Title: World War One timeline.
 D522.7.D45 2012
 940.302'02—dc23                    2013034327

**Editorial Credits**
Nate LeBoutillier, editor; Peggie Carley and Ted Williams, designers;
Svetlana Zhurkin, media researcher; Kathy McColley, production specialist

**Photo Credits**
DVIC: NARA, cover (background, bottom middle, and bottom right), back
cover, 1, 3, 18–19 (back), 19 (right), 28–29 (back), 29 (left), 30–31 (back), 34–35
(back), 35 (left), 36–37 (back), 37 (left), 38–39 (back), 39 (top right and bottom),
42–43 (back), 42 (right), 43, 44; Library of Congress, cover (bottom left), 6–7
(back), 6, 7, 8–9 (back), 8 (left), 9, 10–11 (back), 11, 12–13 (back), 12 (right),
14–15 (right), 14 (left), 15 (right), 16–17 (back), 16, 17, 18, 19 (left), 20–21
(back), 20, 21 (left and middle), 22–23 (back), 22, 23 (left), 24 (left), 25, 26–27
(back), 26 (right), 27, 28 (left), 29 (middle and right), 30 (left and bottom right),
31 (right), 32–33 (back), 32, 33 (top left and bottom left), 34 (left), 35 (right), 36,
37 (right), 40, 41 (left), 42 (left), 47; Newscom: akg-images, 4, 10 (top), 12 (left),
13 (right), 14 (right), 38, 41 (right), Album/Prisma, 34 (right), Everett Collection,
10 (bottom), 26 (left), Mirrorpix, 39 (top left), UIG Universal Images Group/
Mondadori Collection, 40–41 (back); Shutterstock: MAC1, 31 (left), Plutonius
3d, 30 (top right), zimand, 23 (right); Wikipedia, 21 (right), Andros64, 33 (right),
Department of History at the U.S. Military Academy, 24–25 (back), Imperial War
Museums, 8 (right), International News Service, 15 (left), Library and Archives
Canada, 24 (right), NARA, 28 (right)

Printed in the United States of America in Brainerd, Minnesota.
092013      007774BANGS14

# TABLE OF CONTENTS

# THE GREAT WAR

A single death in the summer of 1914 sparked the greatest conflict the world had yet seen. Archduke Franz Ferdinand, heir to the throne of Austria-Hungary, was assassinated in Sarajevo, the capital of Bosnia and Herzegovina. The archduke's murder on June 28 triggered an unstoppable chain reaction of events and pulled all of Europe—as well as Russia, Japan, China, and ultimately the United States—into what became known as the Great War, the War of Nations, and the War to End All Wars. Today it is best known as World War I.

Before the assassination, at the turn of the 19th century, many nations of Europe had been looking for a sense of security and stability amid mounting tensions. Fearful of losing territory and desiring to establish military dominance, these powers formed alliances. Some of the agreements were secret, others more public. Loyalties among nations shifted again and again.

Two sides of a widespread conflict had been clearly drawn by 1914. The Entente Powers (also called the Allies) included primarily Great Britain, France, and Russia. On the other side were the Central Powers, an alliance among Germany, Austria-Hungary, Italy, and the Ottoman Empire. Each side worried about the other gaining political and territorial control.

With the death of Franz Ferdinand, the Entente Powers and the Central Powers seemed destined for battle. One country after another began declaring war. In short order, not just a single part of the world, but nearly the whole world, was at war.

Many Europeans celebrated when war was declared, believing that the conflict would end by Christmas. They were mistaken. The war continued for more than four brutal years, and economic hardship ensued as many countries' resources helped fund the war. Food and other goods were rationed. Women were left at home, adjusting to being alone while thousands of men enlisted to fight. Some children were sent away by parents trying to keep them safe.

The horrors of World War I began early and continued to mount as the months and years rolled by. By the war's end, destruction and despair reigned. The terrible conflict did prove one important point—more clearly than had any conflict before it: War was not something to celebrate.

This book presents an illustrated timeline of the most significant events of World War I, from the causes of the war to the final stages of battle.

# RISE OF POWERS

## Jan. 18

After defeating France and Napoleon III, the separate states of northern and southern Germany merge into a single nation. Prussia is the largest state and has the strongest military. The unification of Germany, with Wilhelm I as its kaiser, establishes it as a dominant power.

Wilhelm I

**1870**

**1871**

**1884**

Germany and Russia move into an adversarial relationship as Germany aligns with Austria-Hungary. Russia's interest in the Balkan states puts it on the side of the Allies.

## July 1870–May 1871

Led by Prussia, the German states defeat France in the Franco-Prussian war, ending French dominance in continental Europe.

## June 15

Wilhelm II becomes kaiser of Germany. He is the grandson of Queen Victoria, who reigns in Great Britain from 1837 to 1901. Born with a damaged right arm—which he blames on the English obstetrician who delivered him—Wilhelm has developed a hatred of all things British. Some historians will point to this as the root cause of his determination to go to war.

Wilhelm II

## May 6

George V ascends Great Britain's throne following the death of his father, Edward VII. George V is a grandson of Queen Victoria and cousin of both Kaiser Wilhelm II and the wife of Tsar Nicholas II. George and Nicholas are also cousins by virtue of their mothers, Danish princess sisters.

George V (right) with Nicholas II

**1888** **1894** **1901** **1905** **1910**

## Nov. 1

Nicholas II becomes tsar of Russia. The latest tsar in the 300-year-old Romanov dynasty, Nicholas has a strong interest in expanding his country's power and influence. His wife, Alexandra, is a granddaughter of Queen Victoria.

## Jan. 22

After a reign of more than 63 years, Queen Victoria of England dies. Victoria's son, Edward VII, takes her place.

Growing unrest in Russia leads to revolutionary activity, but Nicholas II keeps control of his country.

# POSITIONING
# FOR CONFLICT

### Feb. 8, 1904–Jan. 2, 1905

Japan and Russia engage in the Russo-Japanese War, with Japan the victor.

### Aug. 2

The U.S. Army agrees to purchase its first military aircraft, called Airplane #1 and built by the Wright Brothers.

**1904**　**1909**　**1912**

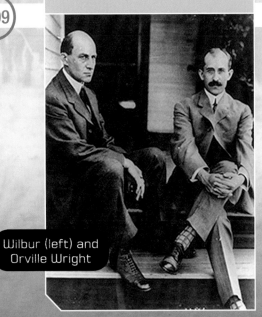

Wilbur (left) and Orville Wright

### May

Charles Samson, a member of the British Royal Navy, becomes the first pilot to launch an airplane off a moving ship. The feat takes place in waters south of England called Weymouth Bay when Samson flies his biplane off the battleship HMS *Hibernia*.

## Oct. 8, 1912–May 30, 1913

Turkey, Greece, Bulgaria, Serbia, and Montenegro engage in the First Balkan War, fighting to grab territory away from the Ottoman Empire.

Battle of Adrianople, First Balkan War

## March 4

Woodrow Wilson is inaugurated to his first term as president of the United States.

1913

## November

French and English navies agree to work together to protect their coastlines from German attack.

## June 29–Aug. 10

In the Second Balkan War, Bulgaria strikes against its allies to gain more territory.

# A SHOT
# TRIGGERS WAR

## GAVRILO PRINCIP

Gavrilo Princip was a young Bosnian Serb and member of the Black Hand. This fanatical Serbian nationalist group was out to kill Franz Ferdinand as he paraded through Sarajevo on June 28, 1914. More than one member attempted the assassination. But only Princip had both the perfect opportunity and a loaded gun. After fatally shooting Franz Ferdinand and his wife, Princip tried to flee but was easily caught. He died in prison of tuberculosis in 1918.

**1914**

### July 23

Viewing Franz Ferdinand's murder as a sinister power play by its despised neighbor Serbia, Austria-Hungary gives Serbia an ultimatum. Austria-Hungary's demands purposely include some the Serbians will never agree to.

### June 28

Gavrilo Princip assassinates Archduke Franz Ferdinand, crown prince of Austria-Hungary, and his wife, Sophie, on the streets of Sarajevo.

### July 18

U.S. Congress authorizes first aviation division within Army Signal Corps.

## July 30

Backing Serbia, Russia begins to mobilize its military against Austria-Hungary.

## Aug. 3

Germany declares war on France. German troops assemble in neutral Belgium, which they intend to invade en route to France.

## July 28

Unsatisfied with Serbia's response, Austria-Hungary declares war against the country, with German support.

## Aug. 1

Germany declares war on Russia. France orders mobilization of soldiers.

# BATTLE
# BEGINS

## Aug. 4

Germany declares war on Belgium and invades. In support of France and in defense of Belgium's neutrality, Britain declares war on Germany.

1914

### THE SCHLIEFFEN PLAN

In 1905 Count Alfred von Schlieffen, a German field marshal, devised a battle plan that involved German forces defeating France with a colossal strike on the western front while holding off Russia with a lighter defensive tactic on the eastern front. When Germany invaded Belgium en route to France in 1914, a modified version of the Schlieffen Plan was enacted—ultimately with little success.

## Aug. 5

The Battle of Liege, Belgium, begins, the first land battle of the war. The Germans enter Liege not expecting much resistance. They are surprised to find that the Belgians, as a defensive act, have blown up the Meuse River bridges both above and below the city.

German soldiers en route to France

## Aug. 6

Austria-Hungary declares war on Russia.

## Aug. 10

France declares war on Austria-Hungary.

## Aug. 12

Great Britain declares war on Austria-Hungary.

## Aug. 16

Liege falls to the Germans. Part of the Germans' success is owed to a new weapon—its massive siege cannon, called "Big Bertha." The shells fired from this thunderous weapon weigh more than 1,800 pounds (816 kilograms) each.

13

# WAR ON LAND
## AND AT SEA

**1914**

### Middle to Late August

German and French forces clash in the Battle of the Frontiers—a series of bloody battles marking the first major confrontations of the war. France uses tear gas grenades against German soldiers. It is the first gas attack of the war.

### Aug. 23

Japan declares war on Germany and plans naval attacks on German forces that have been raiding ships in the Far East.

### Aug. 26–30

Germany bests Russia in the massive Battle of Tannenberg. Though the battle's outcome inspires German pride, it will be Germany's final great Eastern Front success of the entire war.

> *"One of the most brilliant battles in the history of the world had been fought. Germany and Austria-Hungary rejoiced. The world was silent." – General Erich Ludendorff on the Battle of Tannenberg*

### Aug. 22

In a single day, 27,000 French soldiers die in battles at Ardennes and Charleroi.

### Aug. 24

American expatriate and poet Alan Seeger volunteers for the French Foreign Legion. Seeger will go on to fight for the Allies and die in combat in 1916, but not before penning a poem called "Rendezvous with Death." It contains the lines: *I have a rendezvous with death/On some scarred slope or battered hill/When Spring comes round again this year/And the first meadow-flowers appear.*

## Sept. 6–10

The First Battle of the Marne, in France, stops the German advance. Known as the "Miracle of the Marne" by the French, historians will call it one of the greatest critical battles in military history. The Germans' war plan is based on a quick, decisive defeat of France. The First Battle of the Marne wipes out all hopes for that plan's success.

artillery shells in France after First Battle of the Marne

## Aug. 28

The first major naval battle of the war breaks out in the North Sea near Germany's north coast. In the Battle of Heligoland Bight, Britain's powerful Royal Navy seriously outmaneuvers Germany's High Seas Fleet.

# AIR RAIDS AND TRENCHES

## TRENCH WARFARE

Warfare fought in trenches is distinctly associated with World War I. Both sides dug deep ditches in the ground to provide shelter during close-range battles—and a place to recover once the fighting stopped. On the Western Front especially, trenches were used on a massive scale. Trenches saved lives, but both sides found fighting in the trenches dirty, dangerous, and spirit-robbing.

### Sept. 15

The first trenches are dug along the Western Front, giving rise to the term "trench warfare."

1914

### Oct. 19

The First Battle of Ypres, also known as the First Battle of Flanders, begins, engaging French, Belgian, British, and German forces.

### Late October

French scientist Marie Curie begins installing 20 Petite Curie mobile X-ray stations on the French battlefield, for use in helping wounded soldiers.

## Oct. 29

The Ottoman Empire makes a surprise attack on Russia, aligning with the Central Powers.

## Dec. 24

German planes make the first air raid attack on Great Britain, at Dover.

## Dec. 25

In Belgium soldiers on both sides disarm and declare a Christmas truce on the no-man's-land between their trenches.

## Nov. 2

Russia declares war on the Ottoman Empire. Britain and France declare war on the Ottoman Empire three days later.

## Mid-November

The First Battle of Ypres ends, resulting in a stalemate on the Western Front. Trenches are now commonplace along the entire Western Front.

# AIRSHIPS, SUBMARINES,
# AND POISON GAS

## Jan. 19

Germans use motored airships called zeppelins to launch a two-day bomb assault in towns on Britain's east coast. The air raid results in Britain's first bombing fatalities.

**1915**

## Jan. 31

Germans use tear gas for the first time, against the Russians on the Eastern Front.

## Feb. 4

Germans declare waters surrounding Great Britain a war zone. They announce that as of Feb. 18, German submarines will attack and destroy without warning any enemy merchant ship coming toward Britain.

## Feb. 19

Allies begin naval attack on Gallipoli, a mission of invasion into Turkey that will continue for nearly a year.

## April 22

At Ypres, Belgium, the first effective use of poisonous gas takes place. The chlorine gas, released by the Germans, kills more than 1,000 French and Algerian soldiers within minutes of release. It wounds 4,000 others.

## April

Ottoman rulers commit mass genocide over the next few months, deporting and slaughtering an estimated 600,000 to 1.5 million Christian Armenians who live in Ottoman territory.

## CHEMICAL WARFARE

When Germany first used poisonous gas at Ypres in April 1915, the results were horrific. Other nations soon used the tactic as well. The most widely chemical weapon in World War I was mustard gas, which burned the eyes, skin, and lungs, often killing its victims slowly and agonizingly over many days.

The use of chemical warfare was outlawed in 1925 by the League of Nations, an international organization.

# A DEADLY SPRING

## April 25

British troops land on Gallipoli peninsula in the European region of Turkey.

## May 2

Germany and Austria-Hungary begin a massive offensive in Poland against Russians.

## May

Germans begin successfully using machine guns in their aircraft, thanks to a 1913 invention that allows them to fire between the planes' propeller blades at other aircraft.

## May 7

In the Irish Sea, a German sub torpedoes the British ocean liner *Lusitania*. The attack stirs rage among the Allies, including the neutral United States. The passenger ship sinks in less than 20 minutes, with more than 1,000 lives lost, including 128 Americans. Later it is discovered that the *Lusitania* had been carrying 173 tons (159 metric tons) of munitions to Britain.

## May 23

Italy enters the war on the Allied side.

## May 31

German zeppelins terrorize London in the first air raid bombing of that city.

## May 27

The British HMS *Princess Irene* accidentally explodes. Built for Canadian Pacific Railway in 1913, the *Irene* was later acquired by the British Royal Navy to plant mines in 1915. During the *Irene*'s re-fitting, which was being done in a hurry and by untrained personnel, the ship exploded. The final death toll is 352, and wreckage is discovered as far as 20 miles (32 kilometers) away.

## June 6–7

An aircraft flown by Reginald Warneford, a British pilot, destroys a zeppelin for the first time.

Reginald Warneford

# BRITISH
# RETALIATION

## Sept. 18

The German government announces its intentions to end unrestricted submarine warfare after the *Lusitania* incident leads to a diplomatic crisis with the U.S.

## Sept. 25

The British first use chlorine gas against German troops at the Battle of Loos, in France. Gas masks become standard equipment on both sides.

## Oct. 11

Bulgaria enters the war on the Central Powers side, aiding Germany and Austria-Hungary in cutting off Serbia and Russia from Allied forces.

1915

## Dec. 19

Sir Douglas Haig is appointed commander in chief of British Expeditionary Force, troops who received training prior to war for the purpose of supporting France if Germany invaded.

## December

Outdone by the Germans, Allies begin pulling troops out of Gallipoli.

## HEADGEAR

In late 1915 the French debuted the Adrian helmet. Legend has it that during the previous year, a French soldier mentioned to French General Adrian that he had avoided being shot in the skull by carrying his metal food bowl on his head—and thus a new helmet was born. The British "Brodie" and German "Stahlhelm" helmets followed soon after.

# BATTLE GOES
## TO SEA

### Feb. 21

Germans make the first attack on the historic French fortress of Verdun. The French took great pride in Verdun as a landmark, and thus the German attack was an attempt to show disrespect and demoralize their enemy.

### April 9

Canadian forces attack a German stronghold at the Battle of Vimy Ridge. Three days later, and despite 10,000 casualties, Canadian troops are victorious.

1916

### March 22

The *U-68*, Germany's first U-boat submarine, is destroyed by a British depth charge, an explosive dropped into water and detonated at a certain depth. Two months earlier Britain's Royal Navy Torpedo and Mine School had created the "Type D," the first truly effective depth charge.

## April 23

For the first time, the British use a sound-wave emitting device called the hydrophone to detect a German U-boat. Once found, the boat is quickly destroyed.

## May 31

For the first and only time during the war, British and German navies face off in a battle at sea, near Denmark's Jutland Peninsula. Over 72 hours, 100,000 men fight the Battle of Jutland from 250 ships, making it the most significant naval operation of the war. Germany claims the victory but realizes it is not equipped to fight the mighty British fleet except by submarine.

## June 22

German troops reach their high point in the Battle of Verdun. They make no further advances, and by fall, French troops go on a second offensive, making unstoppable headway.

## June 4

Russia makes a surprise attack in Galicia, a region of Austria-Hungary. This move provides the French with powerful backup at Verdun, making it the most successful Russian offensive of the war.

# EXTREME
# CASUALTY

## August

Romania joins the Allies and invades Transylvania, hoping to gain Austro-Hungarian territory inhabited by Romanians. The plan backfires, though, as Germany batters the Romanians, eventually capturing the Romanian capital city of Bucharest.

## October and December

French forces go on aggressive counterattacks at Verdun, winning back nearly all the territory the Germans claimed earlier in the year. Casualties on both sides are extreme. Approximately 377,000 French and 337,000 Germans are killed or wounded. The two sides end the battle in a deadlock, much as they experienced the previous February.

### July 1

Battle begins in France's Somme River Valley to open Britain's first major organized campaign of the war. Called a "baptism of fire" for eager young British volunteers, it turns out to be the deadliest day in British war history. British casualties number 57,470, which include approximately 20,000 dead. The Battle of the Somme will rage on for four months.

### Sept. 15

At the Battle of the Somme, Britain rolls out its first military "landship"—a tank called the Mark 1, designed in 1915.

## Dec. 7

David Lloyd George becomes prime minister of Great Britain.

## Nov. 16

Flora Sandes is wounded in the mountains of Macedonia fighting for the Serbian army. Sandes, who is British by birth, is awarded the Karageorge Star for bravery two weeks later. Though she is not the only woman in the Serbian army, she is the only British born woman to serve as a soldier in the war.

## Nov. 7

Woodrow Wilson is elected to a second term as U.S. president.

## Dec. 29

Rasputin, adviser to Tsar Nicholas's wife Alexandra, is poisoned and shot by Russian conspirators. Somehow Rasputin escapes only to drown in the Neva River. Rasputin was also said to be an acquaintance of the children of the tsar, and a "healer" of the youngest and only son, Alexis, who suffered from hemophilia.

# HINTS OF A TURNING TIDE

1917

## Feb. 24

News of the "Zimmermann telegram" sparks outrage throughout the U.S. and convinces most of the voting public that the U.S. should go to war against Germany.

## March

In Russia civilians and soldiers stage a revolution against the government that results in the abdication of Tsar Nicholas II. Now the country is co-run by the Russian Provisional Government and Petrograd Soviet, a chaotic group of moderates and radicals.

## Feb. 1

Germany resumes unrestricted submarine warfare, hoping to starve Britain into defeat. President Wilson severs diplomatic ties with Germany and warns against further attacks on U.S. subs.

## LAST STRAW

The Zimmerman telegram was a secret message that British intelligence intercepted and decoded. The telegram from Germany asked Mexico to invade the U.S. if American troops joined the Allies.

John Pershing

### April 16

The French launch an offensive against the Germans at the Aisne River in France.

### May 18

U.S. Congress approves conscription and the president signs it into law 10 days later. As a result, of the more than 4 million U.S. soldiers who will serve in the war, roughly half will be drafted into service.

### April 2

Wilson urges some U.S. involvement in the war. Four days later Congress votes in favor of the U.S. entering the war as an "associated power" on the side of the Allies. Brigadier General John Pershing is named commander in chief of the American Expeditionary Force (AEF).

### Early May

The Aisne River offensive ends disastrously, causing whole regiments of French troops to mutiny. An estimated 49 soldiers are later executed for their role in the rebellion. French general Henri Philippe Petain replaces the commander in charge of the offensive.

I WANT YOU FOR U.S. ARMY

NEAREST RECRUITING STATION

## June 12

Greek government officials, seeking Allied support, succeed in pressuring pro-German King Constantine I to unofficially abdicate his throne. A pro-Allies government takes over, and Greece reverses its loyalty, declaring war on Germany and Bulgaria.

## June 13

German Gotha bomber planes hit London in a daytime air raid. It becomes the deadliest bombing of the war with 432 Injuries and 162 deaths, including 46 children.

 1917

## June

The Sopwith Camel, the war's deadliest aircraft, first comes into service. The Camel was a single-seat British fighter plane that was developed from an earlier model, the Sopwith Pup. It features two fixed machine guns that fit through the plane's floor and shoots into enemy trenches while flying fast and low over the ground.

## Late June

The first few U.S. troops enter France as part of Pershing's AEF.

## July

British troops begin to sweep across the Ottoman Empire, and in July, Arabians capture Aqaba from the Turks. Englishman T. E. Lawrence, who later comes to be called Lawrence of Arabia, aids the effort. The Arabians and British gradually gain more and more territory in what becomes known as the Middle East.

## September

German military uses deadly mustard gas against Russian troops for the first time.

## November

The Third Battle of Ypres, begun on July 31, ends after an unsuccessful slog in Belgium mud for the Allies. Germany regains most of its lost territory. In Russia Vladimir Lenin seizes power from the provisional government that has been in place since Nicholas' abdication.

### Sept. 29

The American War Mothers organization is founded for mothers of children who serve in the U.S. military in times of conflict.

### Aug. 2

The Sopwith Pup becomes the first plane ever to land on a moving ship.

# RUSSIA FALLS; GERMANY REGROUPS

**1917**

### November

A second revolution in the same year rocks Russia. The new ruling party is led by Vladimir Lenin and called the Bolsheviks. The results of the revolution will send Russia into a period of civil war and great turmoil.

### Oct. 30

Vittorio Orlando is appointed prime minister of Italy.

### Early November

Germany abandons the fight against the collapsed Russia and moves into Italy to aid the Austro-Hungarians there. Great Britain and France send troops to the Italian front to bolster the defense.

### Nov. 11

Gathering at Mons, Belgium, the German High Command—led by Erich Ludendorff—plans a new strategy for the coming year. The aggressive plan includes taking out Britain and France before the U.S. can enter the war even if it costs the Germans as many as 1 million casualties.

German Generals Hindenburg (left) and Ludendorff

## Nov. 15

Georges Clemenceau becomes France's new prime minister.

## Jan. 8

President Wilson gives his "14 Points" speech to Congress, detailing American conditions of peace. The points include putting an end to secret treaties, a reduction in weapons, independence for several countries, the removal of Germany from occupied territories, and international assistance for war-weakened Russia.

(1918)

## March 3

The Central Powers and Russia sign the Treaty of Brest-Litovsk, which formally ends Russia's engagement in the war. As a result of the treaty, Russia loses roughly 1 million square miles (2.6 million square kilometers) of its former territory, one-third of its population, and a great wealth of natural resources and commerce.

Russian prisoners of war

## Dec. 15

Anti-war movement spreads in Russia after heavy losses on the front. Bolshevik leader Lenin's representatives negotiate armistice with Germany.

# GERMANY
# HANGS ON

**1918**

## March 21

Germany's General Ludendorff launches a powerful Kaiserschlact (Kaiser's Battle) on the Western Front. Called the 1918 Spring Offensive by historians, the all-out German attack hopes to win the war by wiping out British and French forces before mass U.S. troops arrive.

### *April 4–5*

Germans try again—one last failed attempt—to overrun the Allies and take Amiens, France.

## March 23

A morning explosion rocks the Place de la Republique in Paris. The explosion comes from German shells fired from 74 miles (119 km) away by the Pariskanone—a massive artillery gun built to shoot long distances. Despite increasing military weakness, German forces try to seize Paris over the ensuing months and eventually come within 56 miles (90 km) of the capital before being repelled.

## April 21

The German fighter pilot Manfred von Richthofen, known as the Red Baron, is shot down and killed.

### THE RED BARON

Manfred von Richthofen was legendary even when alive. He took his first solo flight after just 24 hours of training and shot down his first enemy plane in September 1916. Known as a calm and deadly killer in a dogfight, The Red Baron made 80 confirmed "kills" before his death, just 11 days before his 26th birthday. His nickname came from the bright red aircraft he flew.

## April 24

Germans finally employ tanks in the first tank-on-tank battle, in Villers-Bretonneux. The Germans take the town but Allies successfully counterattack later that day.

### May

For the first time since the U.S. joined the war effort, large numbers of American soldiers arrive in France to fight back against Germany's major Spring Offensive.

entrenched U.S. soldiers in France

# THE U.S.A.
# ARRIVES

## May 28

American troops, almost 4,000 strong, drive the Germans out at the Battle of Cantigny, France. Despite heavy losses, this first American offensive, supported by intense French firepower, succeeds. The battle proves to the Germans that the American troops are a major fighting force.

## July 10

Maria Bochkareva, a Russian woman who fought for her country and headed up the all-female soldier Battalion of Death, meets with President Wilson in the U.S. Bochkareva pleads with Wilson to have the U.S. intervene in the Russian war between the Whites and Reds.

**1918**

## June

Civil war fully erupts in Russia. The conflict's center pits the Red Army against the White Army. The Reds include Bolsheviks who overthrow the monarchy and hold hostage Tsar Nicholas II and his family. The Whites include supporters of the monarchy and those against the Bolsheviks. Other countries also join and unjoin the battles.

## July 17

Bolsheviks execute Tsar Nicholas II, his wife, and their five children after keeping them on house arrest at Yekaterinburg for more than a year. For years a legend will grow that one of the daughters, Anastasia, may have escaped execution. But DNA evidence eventually proves that legend inaccurate.

Allied forces launch a strong counteroffensive that will defeat Germany in the Second Battle of the Marne.

French troops fighting at the ruins of a cathedral near the Marne

## KILLER FLU

As if World War I wasn't enough, people of the world had to deal with an even more lethal threat in 1918: the flu. The first confirmed outbreak of influenza was at an army base in Fort Riley, Kansas, on March 11. U.S. troops later spread the flu to Europe. By the time it finally died out, the flu had killed an estimated 50 million people worldwide—compared to the roughly 16 million that died in the war.

# WEAKEN

## Aug. 5

Germany carries out its last major air raid of Britain. A British pilot shoots down the command ship over the North Sea, killing the German leader of airships and his 22 crew members. The four other German airships rapidly retreat for home, dropping their bombs in the English Channel.

## Autumn

The many nationalities that exist in Austria-Hungary—Germans, Hungarians, Czechs, Poles, Ruthenians, Romanians, Croats, Slovaks, Serbs, Slovenians, and Italians—begin to fracture. The collapsing Austro-Hungarian Empire urgently seeks acceptable terms of peace with neutral contacts and struggles to maintain the numerous nationalities within its empire. But many of the nationalities declare their independence as separate countries.

**1918**

## Aug. 8

In what is termed a "black day of the German army," Allies accomplish the main strike of the counteroffensive against Germany on both sides of the Somme River.

Battle of Amiens on the Somme River

### September

With Lawrence of Arabia and Arab military forces, Allies push into the Ottoman Empire. Their efforts break the resistance in much of what later becomes the Middle East.

### Sept. 26

The Allies begin their general offensive to take back control of railway lines. At the Battle of the Argonne Forest, U.S. troops participate again in high numbers.

### Sept. 12

At the Battle of Saint Mihiel, troops in the recently established U.S. First Army fight for the first time in numbers large enough to be considered a real army. The German army is severely reduced by the Allies' success.

### Sept. 27

The Allies break the Hindenburg Line in France. The breaking of this German defensive position on the Western Front signals that Germany's defeat is likely not far off.

# COLLAPSE OF
# GERMAN FORCES

"What we demand in this war ... is that the world be made fit and safe to live in. All the peoples of the world are in effect partners in this interest, and for our own part we see very clearly that unless justice be done to others it will not be done to us. " – U.S. President Woodrow Wilson, from the opening of his 14 Points statement

## Sept. 29

With Central Powers collapsing everywhere, German General Ludendorff insists that Germany begin armistice talks with the Allies. Bulgaria surrenders and asks for a peace agreement with the Allies.

## Oct. 4

Kaiser Wilhelm II's loyal ministry resigns. A new German government, led by chancellor Prince Max von Baden, asks President Wilson for armistice. Wilson's reply comes a few days later: For war to end, Germany must pull out of all occupied territory and accept his 14 Points.

Max von Baden, chancellor of Germany

## Oct. 18

An agreement declaring the new nation of Czechoslovakia is signed. Slovaks and Czechs declare independence from Austria-Hungary and join as one state.

1918

Tomas Masaryk, first president of Czechoslovakia

## Oct. 24

The Battle of Vittorio Veneto—Italy's major offensive campaign—successfully drives back Austro-Hungarian troops. Three days later Ludendorff resigns, rejecting Wilson's terms and losing the kaiser's confidence.

## Oct. 28

Disillusioned German naval troops mutiny, refusing to go to sea for one last "honorable fight to the death" that their commander insists upon. The rebellion soon spreads.

## Oct. 28

In Vienna, Austria, German-speaking citizens declare the new independent nation of Austria. The Ottoman Empire completes its armistice agreement and agrees to open its territory to Allied forces. The ethnically Hungarian Magyars revolt, leading to the formation of the independent country of Hungary.

demonstration in Vienna

## Early November

Across Germany, citizens, sailors, and workers revolt, some leaning toward the socialist government now in place in Russia.

# NATIONS FALL
# AND RISE

## Nov. 3

Austria-Hungary disintegrates as an empire and accepts armistice agreement with the Allies.

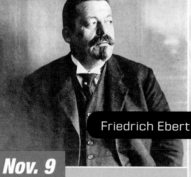

Friedrich Ebert

**1918**

## Nov. 8

The German armistice commission convenes in Compiègne, France, to negotiate the terms of its peace agreement.

## Nov. 9

With mounting unrest throughout Germany, Wilhelm II—who held so much responsibility for inciting the war—abdicates his throne. Pressure to do so, from both the government and the public, is intense. Wilhelm flees to the Netherlands the following day, bringing to a permanent end the German monarchy. Socialist Friedrich Ebert takes over the government from Prince Max von Baden and announces a new German republic. Germany agrees to the Allies' terms of armistice.

## Nov. 11

Armistice Day. At 5:00 a.m. Germans and Allies sign an armistice. Germany agrees to leave all occupied territories and allow Allied forces to occupy all territory west of the Rhine River. On the 11th hour of the 11th day of the 11th month all conflict on the Western Front ends as the Great War officially comes to a close.

## Dec. 1

The Yugoslav National Council formally declares independence from Austria-Hungary and forms its own nation. That nation will take the official name of Yugoslavia in 1929.

1919

The Allies gather in Paris to draft peace treaties, led by the heads of the four major participants (from left), British Prime Minister David Lloyd George, Italian Prime Minister Vittorio Orlando, French Premier Georges Clemenceau, and U.S. President Woodrow Wilson.

## Dec. 1–15

Allies move in and occupy Germany's Rhineland region until peace is established.

## June 28

European Allies sign the Treaty of Versailles, a difficult compromise for the Germans. The U.S. Senate refuses to agree to the Treaty of Versailles, causing the U.S. to come up with its own separate peace treaty with the Germans.

# CONSEQUENCES OF WAR

The Great War was truly a war of the trenches. Men on both sides experienced the grisly reality of being down in a dank, claustrophobic pit, bombarded by the deafening roar of artillery while giant rats scurried through the darkness and the bodies of downed fellow soldiers decayed around them.

The carnage of World War I was unprecedented. In addition to the relative novelty of trench warfare, new weapons also appeared to efficiently destroy human life and alter landscapes. From poisonous gases to destructive tanks and guns to planes raining bombs from above, it was a war of death unlike any before in human history. The World War I death toll has been estimated at 16 million or more.

Thousands of men returned home mentally or physically disabled. Now it was the task of these men and the entire world to rebuild a sense of peace and normality. The world was forever changed, but it had to go forward.

As a result of the worldwide conflict, national borders shifted. Some countries gained new territory, and others lost land. Several nations achieved newfound independence. Women at home had found new independence too. While the men had been away, they had picked up the slack in factories and other working environments. This independence led to women winning the right to vote, first in Britain in 1918, two years later in the United States, and later in other nations.

Also gone was the long tradition of monarchy in Germany and Russia. The war caused huge national rifts in both countries. Russia became a Communist nation, later taking the name Union of Soviet Socialist Republics (USSR). Defeated Germany had to return the territories taken by force from France. Its military was severely restricted, and in 1921 a Treaty Reparations Committee demanded that Germany pay $33 billion to the Allies for the destruction it had caused during the war.

After the war American president Woodrow Wilson called it the "war to end all wars." French president Raymond Poincaré pessimistically predicted that peace would last no more than 20 years. Poincaré was right. In 1939 World War II erupted, a global conflict that proved even more deadly than the first.

# GLOSSARY

**abdicate**—to give up power

**armistice**—a temporary agreement to stop fighting a war

**conscription**—a forced military draft

**diplomatic**—skilled at dealing with others

**dogfight**—a midair battle between fighter planes

**expatriate**—a person who lives in a foreign land

**genocide**—to destroy a race of people on purpose

**invasion**—sending armed forces into another country in order to take it over

**kaiser**—German word for king

**mobilize**—to assemble troops and prepare for battle

**munitions**—materials used in war, especially weapons and ammunition

**offensive**—a forceful military attack

**shrapnel**—small pieces of metal scattered by an exploding shell or bomb

**siege**—an attack designed to surround a place and cut it off from supplies or help

**socialist**—an economic system in which the goods made by factories, businesses, and farms are controlled by the government

**stalemate**—a situation that results in a deadlock, with no progress possible

**tsar**—Russian word for king

**ultimatum**—a final offer or demand, especially one that carries with it the threat of punishment or force if rejected

# READ MORE

**Bausum, Ann.** *Unraveling Freedom: The Battle for Democracy on the Home Front During World War I.* Washington, D.C.: National Geographic Children's Books, 2010.

**Burgan, Michael.** *The Split History of Word War I: A Perspectives Flip Book.* North Mankato, Minn.: Compass Point Books, 2014.

# INTERNET SITES

Use FactHound to find Internet sites related to this book.
All of the sites on FactHound have been researched by our staff.

Here's all you do:

Visit www.facthound.com

Type in this code: 9781476541594

# INDEX